VIRUS

Poetry by

STEPHEN JAMES PITTERS

VIRUS

This book of poems is based on the 2020 COVID 19 pandemic. The poems are about different aspects of the virus and how it affects the attitudes of the population. At the penning of this book more than 200,000 American citizens had succumbed to the virus. Most dying without their loved ones present in the final moments. Heartbreak and sadness consumed many, while others went about their lives as though they were immune to the killer. This collection captures the nuisances and emotions of others to stay at home, social distancing, the wearing of masks, working from home, and most importantly made heroes of those on the front lines at supermarkets, delivery services, nurses, and first responders.

Pitters takes on a confrontational attitude in some of these poems regarding America's justice system. These are raw poems, and they are meant to be.

Prior to this book, Pitters authored four books of poetry, which traced a semi-autobiographically timelines and themes of his life.

Acknowledgments

Halle Kuhar-Pitters—Front cover image
Posie Kalin—musical composition for the poem
"When I Was Six"
Tom Gribble—back cover image

Reflection
Role of the Country

From the well of my soul,
From the seat of my heart,
I am in a country from which my mind departs.
The body quivers, clamors for salvation.
Provoked by the detonating frustration,
fear, rage, and a sense of hopelessness assigned me.
The nation is marked by the sign of Cain
pulsating on every side of its face.
The lesions demonstrate their intents.
The humiliation and reproach some have come to accept.
I am bawling inside from years of physical maltreatment.
Spanked as well by emotional abuse.
The mirror reflects streaming drops
of pellets crossing my cheekbones.
The waterfall increases, the vocal loudness swells,
the howling cascades forming an avalanche that rushes
destroys whatever attempts to interrupt
its push forward.
Sacrifice for many have and will occur
to insure the country's base lawlessness.
Some of those equivocations were noble,
others a blemished encounter
through the palms of unrelenting forces.
Democracy is peering at a nightmare
of unimaginable proportions,
civil rights,

civil survival
for the sake and health of reconstruction.
These impetus and impulses are colliding
rather than entwining to build
profound respectful understandings.
Dying must question the role of its application.
Who are we?
What have we become?
If not lost, surrounded by yesterday's remark,
which perpetually allows some to remain uncivilized
towards his brother,
then castigate the beauty of his sister.

Table of Contents

VIRUS

2020 TONE OF THE DAYS

In the face of life stands terror.
Respect the days of dread
or the horrible virus fiend
will descend and snatch
what is pounding in your chest
putting you in a cold seedy everlasting rest.

GHOSTLY EXECUTIONER

2020, a shower of malcontent
that began as a cold drizzle
then sprinted into a fearful irritation,
detested with its ever-growing aversion.
The rain hacked the morning, afternoon
and loaded overnight with grievance,
snatching whatever valuables existed to confiscate.
The neighborhoods bled a little at a time.
The mean transient with his acid demeanor
shredded sheets, pillows, and heavy comforters.
The grandparents suffered from its heat.
Their feet, back and arms lost their use.
They bent over, coughed, unable to swallow.
Urine cooled them.
Soon, they were left behind in droves.
Day after day their death count increased.
Life for them drifted from the ranks of the living.
The young at heart also were threatened,
and had to forfeit their expectations one by one.
Their youthful sports endeavors slipped into guesses.
Later transforming to a sparse possibility
when first, through eight are not on deck
nor one through five in the blocks.
Weeks went by, leaving the podiums deserted.
Fewer cars and busses adorned the super-highways.
Championships of different types stayed vacant.

Golf spikes, swimsuits, soccer shoes slept in the closet.
Fun, in effect, was done.
What they worked on so hard
for its place in the sun was shelved.
The gatherings handed over the fight to videos
to replicate the terminal run,
the way out for academia.
Superman and Supergirl
had discovered their Kryptonite on earth.
The world was being caged and fleeced of its life forms.
The revolutionary house was burning.
The young would have to reconstruct and remedy
the affliction using cautious measures.
Their time of grief and valor was upon them.
Old trends were not available.
The stout hearted faced a foe mightier
than the sword whose death knell
was presently incurable.
Pain, sorrow, and fear put regression
and commotion on display.
Style and grace with bravery, however,
attended those who could bridge
the gulf of disappointment
and castigate the act of the microscopic adversary.
Each day and night will in time discover a new
opportunity to endure and add arrows to its quiver.
The world is not completely in ruins.
The battle continues; The greens are maturing.
Their motto being,
Resist, Resist be not content to desist.
The world at stake is ours to remake
with valiant knights who will avoid
backpedaling in shame.

ONE TOO MANY

One is too many.
Now 100,000 thousand are taken
and seems almost enough.
They joined the parade of being forgotten.
Who was number one, in the U.S.?
Is she a 57-year-old woman from California?
Who is number one hundred thousand,
a male, female, grandparent, child, husband, wife,
daughter, mother, brother, baby, friend,
stranger, nurse, doctor, firefighter, black, Asian,
Hispanic, Native American, white, from what state?
The person was an American.
Yes, Americans died today, yesterday,
and all the days and nights, three months before.
They were new additions as we began keeping score.
Here and elsewhere we are still number one.
How grand is that, that 100,000 thousand people
crossed the bridge into the abyss of family sighs.
America is broken.
Her stones are piling high.
The bodies are rigid.
They command attention
but heard only a ghostly whisper.
Muted mutterings when alone
feeling hopeless, confused
while silence neared to in-tomb.

They were being claimed at the hand
of a ferocious disease.
America is fractured and ill at ease.
A miserable token unwilling to survive
for all there.
She is unable to coalesce.
Divisiveness has us in a choke hold
with its selfish stupidity that keeps stepping forward
to suppress meaningful sacrifices by those caring
who have unfortunately died,
by an elusive spike driven into their heads.
Crosses mourn them as they sleep.
From a distance, love one's weep.
America, we are in a steep decline.
Our moral compass has become demented,
left far behind.
Certain regulators have chosen not to intervene
and take a dive, instead of performing
bravely for the good hearted.
The crown heads hail the virus with base differences
as the microbe wins the day in the battle of survival.
America divided opened its gate
to the un-seeable death,
whose current death toll shocks.
The previously unknown faces, revealed,
brings verifiable truth to fabricated invention.
Our sensitivity exposed.
Plain old fashion hurt fuming
told its story, ranting and raving with conviction
decidedly adhering to the pandemic emergency.
Lying to the self', hiding in plain sight,
the voices of the silent avoided asking why?
Why did 100,000 thousand citizens have to die?
Excuses rather be defiant than concerned.

Vive la difference, long live the difference
as the result of this lame bias
America's soul sleeps denuded.

DOING MY PART

I was taking a saunter
through beaded breaths.
My wonderings took me
here, there, and everywhere.
The world became my oyster.
I found white, yellow, and purple flowers
along parks, boulevards with swank café's
on which to plant a hiss.
The chatter there flourished.
Laughed in gay spontaneous fashion
on its own behalf.
I grew curious and more involved.
they for a time though,
knew not the impending affliction.
And preceded with their gatherings
in dance halls, ballrooms, at sports stadiums
carnivals and sweet goodnight hugs and kisses.
The need I had to continue traveling would not abate.
So it was, my movements flew from Asia, Africa,
Europe, North and South America
taking vacation after vacation.
I went unnoticed on each shoreline and terrain
that welcomed my quiet overtures
until the terrible deed I spread
reared its virus laden head.
Death for some, then for many a flower

had caused the world to shudder and sink
into an overwhelming loss of life's natural beauty.
Gaunt and hollowness of the citizenry
persisted to address each morning.
Humanity's perseverance waivered in confusion
while body's dried gray and died by the hundreds.
I continued to freelance, rummaging,
intolerant of gender or whomever else lay I before me.
The cadavers of the aged
and some others whose years are close at hand
were at a loss to keep avoiding my cycle.
They tired and stopped; Dropped dead.
I was glad, sincere in my defense
of improper enterprise.
A human of the self-entitled conquerors of the universe
once said, I am just an ordinary bloke
attempting to get along.
Hearing this, I thought,
I was just doing my part,
as a virulent lethal organism killing… likewise.
What was the difference?

CORE OF FREEDOM

Walking away is uncalled for during hard times.
Stand up! Reach out! Be stout!
Take the proverbial bull by the horns,
is the cowboy's code.
Real men made tough decisions
to build the new world order.
Cowards run and hide.
Their names cast ingloriously aside
like trash soon buried
in the whirlwind of forgotten lore.
The rule in the west
is be first-rate
upright and true.
Pull the mule over the grueling passage if you must.
Only children believe nothing bad
or unfortunate will occur
and smiles of reassurances is the cure
for one's predicaments.
The mindset of the west
has done us very well as a nation.
We were propelled forward
in the presence of calamity
and accepted the challenge
from "the slings and arrows
of outrageous fortune"
but took "up arms against the sea of troubles"

Without pride we would be disarmed.
Pride is the alarm for citizens to storm
the castle walls and overturn any enemy,
who seek to unravel the country, whose blood
created its foundational constitution,
its dreams of a better life for all who suffered
the horror of the middle passage,
the trail of tears, wars, famine,
thousand-mile journeys from lands afar
to touch Lady Liberty's torch.
Respect is the core of freedom.
Taking responsibility makes it happen!

AMERICA IS SEARCHING

America is trying to escape from might,
to what is right.
Almost eight decades ago,
a man confined to a wheelchair,
whose first name is Franklin,
practically walked his America
from the grips of the catastrophic Great Depression,
back into the light of prosperity
using his leadership, fortitude, conviction
and love of his country.
America was then able to strut proudly once more
instead of crawling, fumbling in conceit and disrepute.
The late 30's, 40's, was a period,
when the country as a whole
came together with a crystal purpose rather than
petty vindictiveness to achieve its miracle recovery
from an economic war within and a military war without.
America the Beautiful relying on its history,
proceeded to deliver the dream
of another true leader's undimmed vision (JFK)
that led the nation to capture the moon
overcoming great technological odds.
A segment of earth's population
below collectively swooned
when Apollo 11 landed on the moon, July 24[th,] 1969.
America gently planted the red, white sand blue

stretching out the Stars and Stripes on its surface
for those of us below watching, hoping to see them
safely return home. These two illustrious
views commanded our hearts.
The pinnacle of America the Beautiful however
arrived four decades later, January 20th, 2009
with the age of "Enlightened Social Brotherhood."
The longstanding recognizable posture of power
in America at the highest level shifted.
It was seen, and delivered, through a set
of real difference in color. Blackness
held the reigns (Mr. Obama) using style, grace,
family values, and a strong cognitive ability.
He placed the laws of the Republic first,
executed them fairly. Respected constitutional
principles to govern wisely, faithfully.
Rightful judgement was conveyed to all citizens
living in the 50 states and territories equally.
America today, in these times, faith
and trust in Her has dwindled.
Sadness is more visible in the role
of "he who should not be named."
Confusion does not abstain, but maintains
its smudged.
The dreams of the many about equality,
are seldom those embraced by the powerful few.
They prefer gathering more influence
to expand their control, wealth, distance, and leverage.
Having such ruling attitudes in play,
suggests the people, in one form or another,
will most likely suffer, until they receive
the sacrament of Extreme Unction—
the oils and prayers applied at their last rights.

TWISTED SIGNALS

The role of empathy
although appearing doubtful
is still battling with bravery
in its uphill struggle to undo
the extortion planted by the avarice and gluttony
being stamped on the will,
and the soul of the humble.
Considerate common folks
retain their sound, morality.
These everyday spirits find the avenue
to assist their fellows with decency.
Some have allotted their very lives
in this prevention effort.
The Son of the Lord sacrificed Himself
hundreds of years before
that we His children could follow
with love and dedication in our hearts.
There are multitudes the world over
who dutifully respect this ordinance,
while a serious portion rebuke its soulful message,
favoring the opposition "to see no evil,"
hear no evil,
but do as much wanton evil
as benefits their own opportunity.
The U.S. of A. once had a superior moment,
called character.

At present this fabric is damp against a blank wall,
torn, ragged and merely drifting,
shackled by a deviant, pristine abnormality,
whose playing field is chiefly uneven.
Death is calling its own number
with twisted signals.

THE SONG IS DEATH

The standing of America within and outside
its geopolitical zone has fallen way down, way, down.
What it says is a constant spin around.
Truth has lost its head
and cannot find a clean bed
on which, to compose itself peacefully.
Strife and hubbub are the daily turbulences
posting themselves upon segregated pathways.
Belief has no repast for the journey it chooses.
The clouds enveloping life and death thickens.
The light rays strayed deeply into the forest
where wild roving animals scourge each other,
making a body blood count
form a river in which they float,
displaying their tormented suffering.
Persuasive enough to sing the blues.
Known to be America's own generated music
that fashionably celebrates anguish and distress.
Today, yesterday, and tomorrow will find itself
screaming from the four cardinal points of a compass.
Those who court selfishness bring upon others
the massive anemia called the death toll.

THE DOWNER

It is a downer these days they say
subverted on your way,
which means getting old—really old.
Your body withering
carries the scent of a putrid odor,
a piece of rotting ham easily sold,
a dime by the pound to take control.
Its wasting stages accumulate
while you speculate
how to accommodate
the rickety propensities
of a lapsing curmudgeon.
Clarity prefers to infiltrate
and define the locus of his state of mind,
much of it however in a confused
mode of being was left behind.
The last hold on time in-convenient
to unwind. The burial followed suit.

TO REMAIN ALIVE

17

The years ahead spoke to him
without festivity installed anywhere
along its borders.
Too many dark days in succession
were filled with overwhelming depression.
Life seemed a rampage of confusing proportions.
Lifting his head above the cloudy grey marshes
announced only a pause in a robust delirium.
He became the polluted wayfarer
reveling
far beyond the boundaries of make believe.
Stuck aboard an unceasing merry-go-round.
What was before, glorious,
settled for lies, nausea and Tinker Bell's dust.
The tang of the muck
grew into an oozing disgust
for the back end of vitality.
Action once the sparkle enlivening the throne
with capricious buoyancy
soon preferred apathy in which to wallow.
Guidance left him,
and he strayed away
finding the sands of the desert
a hopeless place to hide his face.
The blustery winds were on the warpath.
They tugged at his waning spirit

until The Lord's blessed heart
pulled from him the villainous toxin
opening the gate to veto his lost un-virgin start.
From scratch,
once more in a different way,
came again a fresh and better day.
Such was life,
accorded this opportunity
that we may remain alive
and not lingering, confined,
in hell's decrepit retreat.

THE BEST OF FRIENDS

The pestilence came from the sky.
We breathed its evil message,
before asking why.
The tapping on our shoulders made us cry,
some began to perish.
Others of green years and of ripened fruit followed.
The swelling increased; tears echoed.
Fear challenged each citizen near and far.
Concealment within primary dwelling
raised the trepidation bar.
The multitude hunkered down
leaving the light to atone for the wrongs created.
Weak and worn attracted the ever-increasing storm
that raged by land, sea, and air.
Prayer made its way into the heart of hope.
And slid from there to where humanity's strength
knew it could cope.
Inspiration is a rung on the ladder,
virtue,
integrity,
and generosity uses to scale
beyond the heights of self-gratitude,
low brow corruption,
dishonor and indecency.
The path of the snake
we, as one, with purpose, creativity

and determination interred.
Reposing its venom, beneath the ashes
where only a memory sleep's
of those days of menace.
The sounds of joy had returned
on the lips of children's laughter.
The sight of family's strolling,
painted themselves along the river walks
having long invested communal talks.
Change was here again
ready to brighten the shadows,
its reference, our trusted, foremost friend.

FACE OF DARKNESS

I want this town to turn into me from you
And what was you forgotten from view.
These are the wishes; I hope comes true.
But can you see the evening
transformed into a beautiful park?
Make it; make it a buttery twilight.
The dogs themselves have turned their backs.
Cats, too, knew what to do.
They ran from me to you.
How do we become the better whole
when the color is always steeped in white
instead of righteous ebony hues?
Let the closing sunset paint the proper color,
a darkness compacted—not retracted.
My love for life will not return.
Place it on a mantle in a classical Asian urn.
Permit this noble sanctified jar to be filled
by a previously able body, burned.
Burned into crinkled black layered
grains of sandy dead ash,
before the sun scape returns.
The world should atone for some of its people's
twisted morals and slighted ethics.
One day the untruths of injustice will cease,
and its loathsome perversity
stricken from the light to accept
the certainty seen on the face of darkness.

FAITH LEAKED

I stood far apart from the mob littering
the street with their placards
and roaring voices.
Let them die. Who cares why?
their minds internally echoed.
Those aging souls deserve the great bye- and- bye,
and soon to be followed by the middle-aged
ones who are next in line.
They too will be made to cringe.
There is no vaccine yet to give the people a jolt,
or spin them merrily from hitting the ground.
The serum, a brother to a shot of rum
still is not here to lift their spirits.
The need for its support is now.
Mr. Virus' arrival has my fellow mortals
staring into the barrel of a gun.
They collapse wherever Mr. V goes
like at the Alamo. Inside
the home is the human's last stand.
The Deguello, (no quarter) is being played.
Horror is entering those who would not heed
and resisted the previous rising heat signs.
The devil has mustered a quick march.
The bodies like autumn leaves are
sapped of their once multi-colorful brightness.
Let them die; Don't ask why.

The heartless commissioner whispers on the side
turning his face to sky.
It's their result that they must go meet their maker.
The time had come for simpletons
to visit the undertaker.
Such a lavish homily was issued
by the well healed who lived behind
the white gated communities,
with high iron fences, ringed
by unquestioned comfort.
They have little for a heart
and less compassion from the start
to carry the ill in a cart.
The do-gooders tried
but they, too, under duress died.
Sooner or later with hope fading,
the world suffering will perhaps
only confide in the strong. If Darwin were here,
he would surely have made a dent in this wobbly
tent where some now pay a dear and costly rent.

A GRAND DECEPTION

24

The chant went out one more time,
"We don't care; let others cry."
Let others worry.
They are the ones that should,
those mothers, fathers,
sons, daughters, friends, Samaritans
telling their sad, sad story,
how death came and spread
its morning despicable glory
on the non-cautious days that followed.
And they followed without ceasing,
the breathing and touching
like the stone-cold winter weather
extending its stay
unwilling to thaw the ice.
The agent seeing the opportunity
flowed callously over the bodies of the hosts
making the humans agonize.
How well they suffered.
The biological organism eagerly trounced them,
sparing none who would not give
a good charge to fight its might.
The non -believers waited—
deceived by the thoughts of the ungracious
who knew the unprotected backers
would kiss death.

Come, "Give a close friendly salutation a try."
Let the virus have its way.
Let the grim reaper
hand you a taste of eternal sleep.
You were one of those
that condone deceit.
Their end will answer with a painful, "Oh my!"
choosing to believe as blind fools do
who reject the final agony of being, undone.

THE BOLD AND THE DAMNED

26

The country is in a sordid hole
whose sour depth is expanding exponentially.
I see its soul degrading.
The coughing sounds of its spirit cries out
through the frail voices of the old
being left to their odium.
The stench swallows them.
They are cast aside, helpless to the devices of those
with questionable moral standards—If any.
These self-indulgent monsters have soiled
the many privileges granted the advantaged few,
who clothe themselves in the guise
of the flag. The wise and principled
burned its colors in protest
a mere six decades forgotten.
They respected the core of its freedom then.
Now disrespect is evident and acceptable.
The country is at a loss, in a calamity.
Its rudder broken. The ship of state
flounders waiting to be kissed firmly
over and again by rocks
and the less than secret agents.
Change must bleed for its undeniable future.

THE JUNCTURE

Mother left.
She went.
I wondered why and thereafter cried,
night following night,
Sometimes loudly,
sometimes a sniffle would
mount itself on the precipice.
The ocean below waved its welcome.
I was a child.
I withheld myself, denying the invitation.
Atop the cliff charity beckoned.
The crossroads met me
and flagrantly offered its hug.
The push had only a harrowing collision
against which the plaintiff's accommodation
would absolutely fail.
Be stout.
Be wise.
A weaker boxer would take the dive
and not survive.
The complexity sorrow lends
is an old possession, which garners a place of honor,
and brings together the individual boundaries of
undying love and supreme pain wrapped
in cataclysmic rapid denials.

It is at this juncture I consistently internally disappear
holding inflexibly to a haunting prayer,
she should have remained alive.
My eyes wide open
are filled with a bucket of accusing rain,
arising out of unimaginable torturous pain.

AT ITS BEST

Before the revolution came, we were taken.
Lost to find our own way back.
Confused responsibility was more often
the burden we readily rejected.
Rejected due to the fright its prospect bids us attend.
If we stood, we must go forth and deliver.
Deliver the solution which prompts us to take charge.
Change asked impunity to catch hold
of our souls and be bold.
Rage incensed fired its answer.
We, attacking slavery rose,
and swam
through the dirty waters.
They did not stop nor beg.
Though tired they treaded, bearing down
through the bruising distance,
speaking only a garbled tuneless psalm.
The barking dogs becoming exasperated
let their speech dwindle as well.
Fortitude paid with the flow of warm stale liquids.
None so much as those twenty leather lashes issued
when peeling off black skin.
Their quick short and long strides
unwilling lent the last swallow its defeat
at the edge of the Potomac river's northeast shore.
There liberty flowering slept and slept ever so sweetly.

THE CONTENTMENT

My voice is right.
My voice is nice.
My voice roars and open doors.
My voice is mine not yours.
My voice is how I came to be.
My voice doesn't acquiesce
but knows how to be composed.
My voice clears the dust
that would impede and blind the path I wish.
My voice delivers me to fresh open fields.
My voice is how I feel.
My voice guides my deeds.
My voice is safe; it seeks never to disgrace.
My voice is a friend and leads me beyond boundaries.
My voice upends rigors and transcends.
My voice knows its limits and its heart's beginnings.
My voice listens to the many and the few.
My voice seeks to be happy.
My voice will come to know its end.
My voice, after a time, will face solace.
My voice is peace it need not contend.
My voice crosses the bridges with a vision.
My voice dances with hope.
My voice is the scope of infinity tied to its mind.
My voice will never leave me behind.
My voice takes the foreground by leaps and bounds.
My voice is content even when I'm alone.

LIVE FREE OR DIE

31

There will be a day.
There will be a day
when I can walk freely
and give way to praying
how safety will sacrifice its life.
There was another day, the 4th of July,
which honored
the new country's independence.
We blacks, for four and a half centuries
have waited for ours to arrive.
Puny laws kept shrugging their shoulders.
Lies upon lies came into use and left,
and lives swallowed more and more abuse.
You can't stay here
nor drink water from this fountain.
Red lines cut off where one could buy a home.
Ordinances are still on the books.
Your children are locked up
and unable to play as children should.
The playing field remains uneven to this day.
Though you are born within American borders
or acquired the opportunity to exist there.
The government, which spreads
north, south, east, and west and even off the coasts
sees you as an alien,
and blind to your rights

because your color or accent
makes you a misfit.
"The times they are A- changing," Dylan sang.
They should change for the oppressors instead.
The ones who apply
untold suffering to the body, mind,
and spirit of the disrespected.
Suffering is not an equal opportunist.
It is mainly opportunistic
and decidedly cruel in its conduct and disposition.
The human deportment when linked to a crazy dog
will not suddenly stop doing its harm
without being made to reassess a lifelong
in-grown value system.
Pain and loss severely extended
the diabolical, in-considerate,
intolerant boor his cognitive domain of influence.
There is no more waiting
nor more accepting suffering
or more acquiescing to martyrdom.
Parity and civil rights faced the sword
through broken promises
written in the blood of countless
crucifixions and suffocations.
Much truth exists in the motto, "Live free or die."
These days it is easier to meet death
while walking or running in your neighborhood.
Where do you stand here and now?
Nix living free, let infamy absorb the unjust divide,
which had taken root in the burnt soil.
Who among you will wear the cap of self-respect, nobly…again?

THE MERCY OF GOD

33

The scream that vaulted beyond assurances.
allowed his mettle to waiver in lieu of comprehension.
Hysteria followed the need
softening the pain necessitated
as a mandate for the runaway impulses within his brain,
to gradually postpone these thoughts.
His overly emotional path was determined to improve
the body's functions, to rule
and devour its most elegant attributes,
work,
thrive,
overcome maniacal danger,
and grow to reach its august mountain.
The acceptance of a spiritual love
cloaked in empathy and compassion.
Authenticated through the glory of living
given by the mercy of God.

THE GRIEVANCE

I was set adrift to float upon
the wide-open blue ocean
without the means to ferry myself back to shore.
What I must do should have purpose,
and reflect what we labored industriously to acquire
rather than relinquish the honor of the past
we bled to denounce. Is there
a steadfast location for the
likes of black citizens apparently abiding
temporarily within the confines of these fifty states?
It is not a myth, but an afflictive ongoing reality
crystalized and maintained for our brain to detain.
We who inhabit the color black
are strapped to its duress deep inside
our consciousness where we continue
to walk alongside the appalling – grievance
on the toll *Road to Perdition*.

AULD LANGSYNE

I have been sitting and standing around
for a few decades.
Now my hands and feet are getting cold,
while I sit pensively on the throne
calculating my approaching limit.
Old-man death has begun sliding through me.
He is searching for a place to camp.
He is making me feel damp.
I think he wants to take my energy
and revamp my landscape.
Cut my playing fields.
If he thinks, he has me on my heels.
He may be right but otherwise not tonight.
The heart is pulsating loudly.
The mind still at bat stays in the game.
Been planning for this something,
something to leave behind—
the poetic song of "Auld Lang Syne,"
the record of my life
with all its times emotionally remembered
have yet to whiff at the curve, a call strike three.

REGRESSION—SEEING DEATH

Have you ever grappled
with a sudden rolling bloating feeling
coming up into the pit of your stomach?
As it ascends there is a slight choking
when it reaches the pit in the base your throat.
The taste of lime is expelled from the nose
and mouth. The blood in the veins
pushes against the temple walls.
The pressure raises to a high level.
You can feel it on the skin of the forearm.
The eyes experience an intense compelling
Swelling, and they water slightly.
The need to cry almost erupts.
Sorrow begins its march throughout the mind.
The reason is unpredictable.
The regression asked for a thought.
Loss answered the call
of the many experienced.
I felt my mother's death
registering again against
the farthest wall within me.
I enter convulsions.
The waterfall soaks me.
My back sweats; my neck hurts with pain.
I want to hold back the coughs.
They swell rapidly, audibly.

Cupping my mouth, I suppressed my breath
bit hard on my teeth.
I exhaled through the nose, then lips three times.
My chest collapsed.
I gulp slowly easing the rush
that had been ricocheting
around the inside of my head.
Rising to my feet, I felt refreshed.
The sorrow subsided.
The tears abetted. The image
of a child crying left me for a while.

LET'S GET MOVING

I hear my anger marching—
marching to its independence calling.
Calling me to reach a blessed home.
 Egypt is in bondage.
"Martin, you left me!"
Danger has taken your truth to its grave.
I still labor above and beneath
the blood-soaked soil after being taken
from my far-off land.
The years without privilege calls me.
I have no more sacrifice to give.
I must take immunity with raw power
or die impotent consigned to a misused pity
willing to laugh uncaringly.
Moses has not returned with his staff
to open the Nile waters as before.
Miracles, what are they these days?
What must I do? I feel daggers
running me through.
They are written in self-seeking ignoble perjury.
Determined to impale my centuries old
wounded spirit. I must swim strongly
to another shore though the river is cold,
muddy, and swift.
The strength of my resolve moves me onward.
A place awaits absent of abasement.

The new Pharaoh in his time scalded
the remnants of nature's sparkles
searing it with impunity's disrespect.
The challenge had to be answered.
The sycophants maintained their posture.
Our country lost its under pining.
"Harriet," I feel your dauntlessness.
Death is the only salvation we must embrace
when restraint fall to its knee.
Let us walk fleetly and shirk this wounding weight!

NOT A PERFECT DATE

History moves.
Man stopped improving,
reforming his conscience
by not informing its belief system
regarding the errors he made,
which would have transformed
the bitter hatred long residing there.
How does your world feel today?
Did you wake up to pray or just say,
"Who cares," before creeping back into
the lackluster regions of sleep?
Is life for you warm and steady
exempt from distraction?
Change is stalking you like a mentor
just about to call class to order.
Time for learning as always been at hand,
otherwise we, as a nation,
will continue securing our damning ways.
This incarcerating, protracted behavior
is still ticking at the expense of The Brothers.
Black is black.
White is not Lancelot a knight in shining armor
only The Man extracting his grand plan of action
from which, there is no escape
if blacks wait for a date with his
goodness,

tolerance,
and charity.
Dependence on another's sense of fairness
will surely keep us from flourishing,
especially when justice is not only blind
but arrogant and vain.

THE GUILLOTINE

What can I do,
when the silent verdict approaches bigotry
 and sticks a knife into my chest?
Shame on me if I will not instinctively resist.
Should it be death or the dishonor,
which finds me cringing underneath
narrow-mindedness.
The cost is high. Others un-spared.
Illness will gravely wash the face of the nation.
The tempo is set in the name of ending life
like a monstrous cattle stampede
crunching the fertile sod.
We failed at first to thwart the beast.
The yeast however kept spawning,
expelling snake like venom,
which took the old,
young and in-between.
Its thundering march
crippled into darkness the weak and helpless.
The voices of those who would be martyrs
began to roar.
Their sacrifices made its presence known.
They came from everywhere and showed their love
to their brothers, mothers,
sons, daughters, and friends.
Good Samaritans rescued strangers

with their own lives.
The fight went on and on
as days became months.
Mortality filled the count higher and higher.
The open-hearted,
charitable obliging souls,
held fast against the challenge
facing self and neighbors next door.
Obliteration would not retreat,
nor was it indiscreet.
Its boldness stripped from some their humaneness,
while from others' acts of great courage
grew and grew as they faced
this uncommon vicious viral test.
We all in the bleakest time yesterday,
today and before tomorrow
would come to know that compassion
rather than selfish narcissism's
prevalence is inadequate.
The heart knows its calling
and sees how consideration will salvage us
from this catastrophic guillotine.

SIX YEARS OLD

When I was six years old without knowing
how sick mom was, she died.
Until today, seven decades later,
I sit here staring at a photo of her soft caramel face,
short brown hair, slightly full lips,
rounded cheek bones, narrow strait nose.
She was totally calm, serene.
I knew immediately to love her.
How could I not?
Mom was mom.
Dad remained attached and never remarried.
He hid his feelings, trying to be strong
as one day passed another day
and night after night,
a sniffle here and there
from midnight to sunrise was herd.
I shielded mine playing silly games
as a child will. The malignant growth
kept making gains, diminishing,
gnawing her body's reserves.
Her lungs were losing their puff.
The young family tried sparing themselves
with will power, faith and courage as they should,
while she dwindled on the bed
across the white wrinkled sheet.
I had little knowledge; she was fighting

a desperate battle attempting to ward off
the devil's unwanted piercing stopover.
Her creamy visage maintained the subtle gleam
she refused to withhold.
I hope she could retain her sun.
The evil snake however had her back peddling,
like an army in full retreat.
The coughing tore her lungs.
She winced.
The ghastly, raspy sound
screamed murder off her tongue.
Moving onto her left side, she became quiet.
Stillness filled the pale chalk white room.
The verdict announced itself.
We were not ready for her exit.
I should have remembered
how mom looked,
but at six, who knows any better
except to suddenly cry and cry.
Confused at feeling empty.
Hope the mutter of dreadful unease,
conflicted overwhelming terror.
The need to run, jump off the riverbank,
and swim to the other side.
None such events happened.
She remained still—never standing up.
Days afterward, my face looked
into the black coffin at the church.
I stared at her beautiful face.
It was the final time.
What there was around me was displaced.
I felt myself a brick at six but totally weightless,
emptied, morning, noon, and before night fell.
Distracted, I did forget after a time.

We as a family left her emotionally undiscovered.
Loss deteriorates following the interior regret
until the key, a visiting moment awakens,
reestablishes the value I no longer put away.
I was grown. Her picture sat there—her beauty
fully understood.
My love for her clarified, realized, magnified,
sedately imbedded in my bosom.
I felt pleased knowing instead of crying.

THE AFFECTED

I am sad for my country.
My stomach hurts.
I stand holding onto a steel lamp post.
About me there is a calm.
The silence are my own thoughts moving slowly.
I feel them. They are confused.
They want to release the nature of absurdity.
Loss has come and is taking its roots
like cold raindrops upon my head.
I prefer going inside. I am making it there to hide
from the slow growing smarting.
Rage is bitter. It injures and burns.
My mind has started instructing me
with a strange agony.
Though not depleted, it wears down
my emotional solvency. Before me
I am faced with an onrushing quandary
imposed by a bleak tribulation
lashed to the country I like less
than when entering its splendid shores
many decades before.
Today on this rainy overcast Tuesday,
my tears join the rain.
My joyless feelings I can explain.
America's brightness is but a glint
fading under a boatload of desperation,

riding on the rim of object
longstanding violations, she has chosen
not to withdraw. In each century,
the outcome has resulted in
expressed social upheaval, murder,
hunger, disease, and callous disinterest
borne primarily by people of natural color.
Yes, the crime is an illegal transgression
to their body and soul.
No remedy has yet occurred
to halt this four- hundred- year malicious constancy,
which is lust for and to cultivate unlimited power
in the control of the privilege minded,
soiled worms who eat all they can.
Wherever they roam leaves me in a fit of annoyance.
What is good seems to be absolutely misunderstood
and underserved. This mindset is old
indeed, and beholding to the devil.
He has been living on many shores like these as well.
The quest of humanity appears to lie
in deplorable behavior, selfish aggrandizement,
link to the heinous harm
that festers killing the values our Lord asked
us to display, respect, brotherhood, empathy,
mercy, love, and goodwill.
Too much, however, for the sum
of His collective parts. America in its years
has wallowed in the filth of the masses—
the seediness of deprivation,
the narrow-minded execution,
cast upon the defamation of the black character
who sought inclusion that has still been refused,
barred, their guts ripped apart
sold as justification for a sordid satisfaction.

America lived in darkness in the past.
America again has attained a level of mediocrity
and will continue to debase its quality
for the sentient purpose of money, prestige,
personal advantage, and gross power.
These diseases have no curative vaccines
except the removal of those affected.
Until then, America and I cannot
be the best of friends I still hope for.

COMPLY

The world reposes between
gentle day and calming night.
Much of this longitude and latitude,
my will opposes in its address
whenever thoughts of mom and dad
both in eternal quiet yanks at me.
My sprit plunges. I bleed
the onslaught of cascading whimpers.
Thoughts scramble running without any certainty.
Ghosts become real and the ordeal returns to haunt
the tender lair I built, which is wavering emotively.
I can only ask, what on earth has happened?
The phantom of pass despair is here.
His hatchet hurled damages my heart as before.
There he sank bloody teeth attacking deepest love.
Formerly, I always ran to it for cover.
The barred gate is ripped open.
I hang on barbwire's incoherence, again.
What I know to be true is,
I have lost touch
with the two most important spirits
that gave me the greatest sense of validity.
They are gone; mom and dad are dead!
Dead to this world!
Their absence of happiness is
my backbone nearly broken.

I have neither diamond nor emerald
to bring sunshine as an assistant
for the lonely rainbow's much needed delight.
Friends even now are few.
I am charged to seek the neighborhood tavern
and pluck from it a bit of relief for my fallen stars.
The world in me is mislaid and over-thrown
by sorrow's impinging demand.
Deficit has me vomiting over the porcelain sink.
Mom and dad are nowhere real. I can, however,
feel the grumble. My heart is harmed, again.
I wish I didn't exist in this world.
My desire longs for red and yellow roses
and a spark of daylight,
bright extremely blinding daylight
to burn through any shadow hanging about me
and will kiss the umbrella of the great blue yonder
uplifting the need for energy's boom.
In me their discerning thoughts and faces
both address and condense me.
I say hello to them, adding, "Mom and Dad,
the world can only be wonderful when you are nearby.
"Come back again please be not shy.
"I need not ask why,"
to their tear-jerking visit, I surely will comply."

TENDERIZING (SOMETHING YOU NEVER THINK OF)

I chased many strands of life
until there was no more to be had.
When that time came, all of me lay sad.
I was relieved.
Glad.
The torture had ended.
Glad the rumble and stumble
and the rest of local experiences were abandoned.
Dedication contacted me one fateful night.
My usual response was to fight any strife
by clutching its throat,
exhorting what I should believe being black
living in a conflict ridden, daily boiling,
imperfect, grating, disaster, called The United States.
I wasn't trying to stop.
It arrived when I ran out patience
and couldn't think anymore.
Unable to talk to myself.
Too much to keep inside from someone,
Too much was real,
Too much requires
one to be stronger than steel
and changed how he feels.

Perchance that was the crown of the absolute deal.
The fulfillment of death's implosion,
leaves the farmer's body as the means
to tenderize his dry Midwest corn fields.

53

THE PILE

I was a wisp of a man
who once began, then fell behind
and couldn't catch up again
in twice the time.
To inaugurate, a start made me at once late
and later yet
when attempting to advance shy of assistance.
The profuse corrupted distinction
created a lack of concern for order,
producing failure as the mantra involved in waste.
Its aroma simmered, waited, and instructed
his followers to revere their demand for nothingness.
Pigs have skins that become oil,
grist for the fuel that failed to purify
the sanctity required to scale the next paramount
spiritual undertaking; from an elevated vantage point,
I dropped the teasing torch.
Fire chastised everywhere.
The dungeons where doused in screams.
The guards saved themselves being safely detached.
The prisoners however expired
and found another kingdom
in which to satisfy their wasted life.
Philosophy remained behind to argue
in defense of liberty deplored
and restitution ignored.

It took everything to undo,
to uncover the passage avoided.
The one which led from glare to gloom.
The smoke had so clouded the room.
Bones retired relinquished their small parts
placed in a cream color pile together.

GRIEF

We strode into a difficult time easily remembered.
Agony spread itself freely, speedily.
A visitor deforming weak minds
and delicate bodies, which exploded
like a firecracker on a July summer afternoon.
The dwellers dropped and folded
into timbered gutters, where they lingered.
Divorced from life's polite estate,
restrained from perceived grandeur.
Blandness endured, however.
The train flashed to deterioration,
keeping up its march pilfering a dulling egress.
Change persisted in its transformation,
exceeding the blackest night's intrinsic alteration.
Change wouldn't change
like a deception nourishing a disease.
Selfishness walks its own way
following death's claws
that chose today to flaunt its will on those
most disposed from sea to shining sea.
They and families surprised…. grieve.

MY SONG, MY NEEDFUL SPIRIT

57

We each have a song.
Some are short.
Some are long.
Some are weak.
And others strong.
Some take us far
while others not far enough.
The soft melody in some, nicely overcomes,
we beam expressing amusement.
The rough tones parades through others,
mock the sun and stars,
curse the miracle which celebrates God
but embrace the devil, spreading his seed,
his message that harms
the heart and minds of the innocent,
applying its resonance,
they lose faith and are wasted.
The stress makes them become a thick,
slimy, sludge, stuck on the bottom of the river
where life's dreams are silenced with the hush
of their song which prefers to be prolonged.
"Hark the Harold's Angels" wanted to sing"
But there was no glory nor a king
only the cessation from he who developed a void
having misplaced the tracks of his will.
Without something there is nothing.

No peace in a world for those who are at a loss.
They labor hard and are losing the war
to gain a proper freedom to portion
another satisfying painless day,
in the presence of their needful spirit
singing to their crucial wanting mind.

BEFORE DEMAND

In the backdoor of my life, I use to be a dasher,
A masher,
A crasher,
A slayer, then I prayed long and hard.
Asked the Lord
for a positive way for me to shine,
see, and make finer choices,
rather than merely the use of easier devices,
to obtain quick sampling results
at the expense of another's goodness.
I questioned my inner and outer areas
where the mean monsters lived.
I challenged their access to my will.
Spent hours in gloom facing emotions squashed,
attempting to avoid the backlash.
Blind denial led me on
like a farmer sowing his fresh seeds row after row
until the locust of struggle came.
First the heat dried the topsoil, strafing its life.
The raging winds followed
and stripped what was left of the surface.
Torrential rains flooded and drowned fields,
saturating subsoil of their nutrients.
Belief and change held on,
took hold of the nightmare.
Stopped the adversity.

Growing up is no elementary task.
Getting along with difficult demands,
working with the outcome,
fashions the sculpture
through the holder's innate vision,
as Michelangelo did for his David,
bringing forth absolute beauty to life from marble,
free of doubt, chinks, or mimics.
Legacy resides in alterations before demise.

BURN BABY

Silence crowded our boarders.
Silence walks over our homes.
Silence crucifies the bodies of young and old.
Silence mangles the respect we had for the roots
that once bore the fruits we honored,
integrity, fairness, equity.
Before us, nothing was treasured
only distilled, stolen for private gain.
Maimed by slavery bought
 in the modern world of abject contempt.
Can we return to form?
A reasonable assisted one,
where truth does not hide?
Where brotherhood marks the love for our neighbor
rather than a self-induce hatred for his skin or
or where his accent begins?
What there is that surrounds us,
we need not obliterate.
What taught us, wrong is right,
bad is good; are the things we wanted
and took as a matter of course.
In that we overdosed.
We died in shame,
becoming rotten to the core,
a disunion, a sordid rebellion,
of parting ways.

The world about our toes was not soft enough.
Upon it we pressed hard,
leaving heal imprints,
mashing our deeds down,
like the scars of euthanasia.
Unaffected we didn't care to discern.
We lit the fire and shouted, "burn baby burn".

GRANT HIM PEACE

63

The world is not flat
but most know that its festive feasting
is slow at keeping the round ball
continually spinning.
The dizzying clip flipped him over and over.
How he is and wished to remain
cannot be.
The haze became thick
and common ways are removed.
His life's conduct is wrongfully affected.
He pushed forward in space to a point
far beyond, however now, he has chosen not to return.
The grass was indeed greener on the other side
of contentment.
Self-assurance and a loss of contact with the Holy Spirit
gathered for him the boastful ego of a false prophet.
Lucifer mounted himself on a mountain top
and called to His sheep below.
They came like a pacified herd
eager to discover a new light,
a new meadow in which to graze.
They sat pleasantly, raising their voices
with willful devotion and allegiance.
Safety was without care,
enthusiasm reign in abundance.
The future seemed an unlimited possibility,

before suddenly moving aside, backwards.
A tremendous tide of discontent
in his purpose had stripped him
deceitfully, blindly in bits.
The wizard was swept from the land
like a malfunctioning gland.
His hand and feet shriveled.
Deformed he is unable and incapable
even to compose the sign of the cross
as the means to recapture his life.
Dear God grant your shepherd, his final peace!

MALADY

I am still trying to catch sight
of where I am going.
I don't know what fondness is.
I hear it has been traveling overseas on
majestic ocean ships enjoying a vacation
on iron grips that is how rich folks calmly exist.
I saw a girl today.
Her ebony hair displayed a courtly sheen.
Her svelte hips were engaged in shapely blue jeans
that jumped all over her.
She appeared ordinary
but inside I felt her beauty professing
the makings of a queen.
Her friendly face made me confess the evils
my poor heart declared.
She was altogether true-blue.
Evil nevertheless from within me
cast upon her a severe mildew
that would serve to separate us,
our growing, governing hearts with disgust.
The near future between now,
and years ahead promptly turned into acid.
The hurt was shocking.
She bled out emotionally in sad distress.
My confession was overwhelming.
Her sweetheart could only refrain and chastise,

swelling under the strain the lies hammered
into her mental capacity.
Further sunny days stalled
preferring to hand them darkness instead.
The sourness grew; distrust radiated in every glance.
There was no counterbalancing their ship
today nor tomorrow.
Leaving, profits a plausible outcome
from life alienating malady's
penned by the tongue.

THE GLARE

67

What happened were prickly scenes
moving here and there.
The rear of people dashing in despair
with tiny portions of what their lives donated
as entertainment to fill their belly's daily demand
to its brim. Being hungry from the night before
is a constant chore the mean streets adore.
I lived life on a dime representing, "who cares".
The wide open, world for those struggling is dim.
It trims the fat off the bones,
mocks the sensitive fiber, I try to uphold.
My essence is losing molecules of animation.
I have begun moving aimlessly.
I see only vast mounds of sand
stretching endlessly before me.
I am glancing at a speck.
The steps I take are slow.
The image appears to be diminishing from the rim.
It is fuzzy.
The heat waves increase.
My tongue swells.
I choke.
Spit left my mouth in a curse.
The clothes on my body has sores,
holes everywhere.
Caring is life closing the door

of what I can't value anymore.
The self has drifted into powder
without its glare
to which I am evermore, unable to adhere.

SLOWED INSISTENCE

69

Oh! ye, moody river,
take me from the green banks
into your cold distress,
that I may seek forgiveness
for the reverse significance
my years accrued.
I trudged along like a mule.
I festered rather than flourish,
lost in a storm where life's soul
had no appeal.
Parts of me slowly became disarmed.
I withered and felt a distant quiet
for what remained in me
of time's depleting tragedy.
To its whimpering call, I made a bona fide charge
knowing full well I must ring death's devious carting.
I was a child once but now I am thankful this late
to have shed the terminal anguish
plucked from tomorrow's slowed insistence.

THE ENVOY

When love can't find its way,
a pound of grief is here to stay,
displaying, whatever slight it deems necessary.
Life inwardly is drowning
along the shorelines of sweet Americana
Pallets crowd and stain the walkways
were bodies now reside on the morning dew
Someday like today as the corpses
still strewn by the thousands,
No heavenly chorus
will add their mourning anthem.
The smell of burning bones coughing
is the only tribute to a divided ill-advised temple.
Lewd laughter by itself in the confessional
addresses the priest
before he makes the sign of the cross
hoping to bar
the devil from his further envoy's duty.

A LIFE REMAINING

People are as they become,
withholding acceptance,
of others equally striving to attain
what the world provides through dreams,
effort, and over-arching, tireless hope.
The scope of which is unlimited.
Each path that encircles the globe attests
to the creation of future's incarnation.
The strokes taken weigh
heavily and require continued
application mostly through combat
with autocrats, bosses, oppressive leaders
having narrow ideals and overloaded dubious morals.
Fearlessness is strict and does not shy from engaging
the presence of disaster's voice
seeking to rule absolutely over another person
hopes. Agreement with all there is
contributes sensitively.
There is enough of everything,
for everyone, on the planet.
Let's get moving and not deny nor disengage
for the sake of malicious greed, we put in our way,
if we hope to stay here in good health
and have, remarkable, fantastic days
and splendid ways
in a life, now only partially remaining.

YEAR OF LIVING FEARFULLY

72

2020, the year life took itself
to the stratosphere of phobia.
Misfortune ran rampantly through the streets,
and alleyways of towns, villages,
and major industrial cities
on the arm of the lucid virus.
Whomever trespassed,
his interest recklessly consumed.
He brought the tide of undoing
into any home or bedroom available to his thirst.
Vulnerability swooned,
when the icepick stuck hundreds, thousands acutely,
mercilessly.
The human stay on the "celestial body
orbiting the yellow star" was indifference
stopping to chat.
The anomaly accommodated
whatever handout was obtainable
throughout the year.
So it was, that people were taken,
stolen, burned, buried,
left in the rearview mirror, choking on love.
Abnormality nevertheless persisted
almost blindly towards its acquisition.

THE AFTERMATH (KRISTIN)

There will be more dying,
more quietly sobbing,
mentally distracted from their days ahead,
swaying abstractly,
offering anguish its toll
for their broken road.
The large road sign said,
"You have now entered the Town of Goodbye."
population, Growing.
Your heart will ache the longer you remain.
The longer you question your loss.
Remorse will haunt and taunt.
The voice of love will be torn apart
each time it sings, calling to him or her,
"To please stay, don't go;" "don't leave us behind"!
Anger will take over.
Irrational pain will continue with its debate.
The aggregate grief compelled to achieve
in time a total collapse.
The saint had been stripped of his wings
by evil's deadly attachment to his body
but not his soul.
To this family, he filled the room with happiness
and triumphant jubilation.
He was the bedrock on which they stood,
the values all there in, understood.

Work hard, be just, kind,
respect your fellow human being.
His was the face from which the sun shone
and the night made its peaceful departure.
He would want us to keep trying,
trying not to merge with him dying.
Our ailing emotions resisted though we knew,
he could not remain above earth anymore.
His purpose was us, his family.
The battle call we hurl back to him
is love today and the next day our eyes open
with dedication standing strong
in God's holy hand.

FEARING WELFARE

75

I dreamt of the gnarling sound of extinction
whose two hands pressed themselves
tightly upon my neck.
The oxygen within was stifled,
incapable of releasing itself.
My temple hammered.
Red blood squeaked through the ears.
I wished for a stay of execution.
There was no absolution permitted.
The glory of the church denied
any self-ordained mutilation.
Should I choose to hang head down
by my own statute of limitation?
Dreams are the blind fury
a haunted deposition purposefully adopts
and to it attaches itself,
like an allure eating the heart
fearing its crippling, defying, welfare.

A PROFILE

A longtime ago
what some of us started was how,
we saw ourselves
and what we chose to do
to execute our own purposes
to capture the benefits befitting us.
Our views became the zest
of our quest for life at its finest
or advantage without experiencing
consequences, whether right or wrong.
The mindset of this nature developed through
an extreme preferential attitude
based on scorn and entitlements often given
for self-affecting internal trivial hunting.
Objects have premier value
and are to be acquired by whatever means available.
The rationale resided in the home of lying, cheating,
and stealing for one's aggrandizement.
Demeaning others profusely
is the path their excuses develop to hide behind
while they pilfer and purloin
using misdirection to abscond with the goods.
The most valuable object reflects in the mirror.
Conceived as being right.
The justification ensued
to substantiate any inscrutable acts

of fact or fiction.
An entire psychological foundation
is designed to create pathways
leading to continuous advancement
at any expense for others.
Degradation and affronts
are calculated as acceptable
to these over-esteemed animals.
"I have, but you will be kept from achieving
any significant port of entry"
are the thoughts of privilege.
"The good life is for the few not the many
regardless of their sense of fairness".
"Darwin knew this." We are here to execute it
and capable by managing the reigns of disruption.
What ultimately will present itself to the multitude
is grief if the fashionable hooligans
burn and sack villages, towns, and cities to the ground.
And allow bodies to stink in the open, stone cold dead,
meanwhile escaping with a crown of jewels
fitted exactly for their heads.

DIVINE COLLABORATION

There is a wrinkle in my mind
that allows all things to unwind.
I see green stars,
which traveled from deepest red oceans afar.
These quantum strides ride within kinetic waves,
morphing into galactic gasses
whose tinctures draw
marvelous twinkling canvasses
so ornate, Maestro Michelangelo
di Lodovico Buonarroti Simoni himself,
would encounter such a herculean protest
to reconstruct this pigmentary grandiose design.
He with his talented artistic mastery
and with extensive time
may conceivably been able to paint
an ideal pictorial homage for the eyes
of divine collaboration.
Inspiration may not always be fulfilled.
but with the will lifting, imploring imagination's thrill,
reality maturing is led to conclusively comply,
therefore, ratifying the majestic lights
deemed the cloak,
honoring God's heavenly commonwealth.

IDLE SPECULATION

What dismay occurs these days!
The quest for happiness is far from gold.
We are racing, becoming old.
What a bore!
Our time is busy dying.
Our years are closer prying,
without gratifying
while getting us to greet denying.
We need some shelter.
The swelter is out of control.
Confusion is yelling.
There is no pardon.
What was said must be,
and done.
The trouble is.
Lives of too many are piled at the dump.
Leaving shame and disaster a camp for rashes
The boundary between life and death
is linking rather than barred.
The prayers of the sheep
keep asking forgiveness
from the orchestrating devil,
bent on delivering the shakes
and bushels of misery.
A painfully bad situation is getting worse.
We must slow the movement

of this bloating catastrophe.
Where is the miracle juice?
or the magic pill needed to stop the drilling
killing the body, soul
and totally consuming the spirit?
Must we bestow our flailing history
to absolute futility? Could my emotions
be bordering on mere idle conjecture?
Spare me the aimless speculation!
I have a cave carved out beneath the house floor.
Freedom is waiting there to plant me in dirt if it must.

THE MENACE

The world conveys
a contaminated impression today.
Each continent displays
rotting goods on its tray.
The hunt for happiness has gone astray.
The gay blue, green, yellow, red colors of the rainbow
in our life was abandoned,
when death unleashed its towering presence
upon the acres we use to cross.
The deadly merchant put us at a loss.
What had we left to say,
careening backwards day after fleeting day.
The sun rising on its own tried to ward off
the crawling shade of darkness stalking the coastline
with its gripping fingers of silent cessation.
My world shrunk the night.
She ignored not returning home.
The bitter shrew to life
was no speeding iron car's bolted fender
nor grim bullet to the brain
but the imperceptible, almost invisible,
microscopic agent,
who adjusts his deadly presence into the gel
of his newly found oyster.
God and Satan's domain broke loose.
The human inhabitants addressing

the various surfaces of the planet
suddenly diminished.
Death is a wanton menace.

LAND, SILVER, AND GOLD

The country, hitherto known as the center of the world
has been slipping and sliding lately
easing and hiding under the tutelage
of dastardly carpetbaggers.
They swindled land, silver, and gold.
Undermined and rewrote the laws to their benefit.
Castrated the helpless and the hungry.
Disposed of those who were without substance
to defend themselves.
What could be taken; they swallowed with immunity
calling it Manifest Destiny.
Stealing couched in a grand design.
The land once innocent was weakened
overrun and overturned by these immoral locusts.
Men and women whose belief systems painted
their non-visual likeness,
"animals," "savages," "dogs" unfit to persist
along-side what mankind is
and has proven themselves in their own minds,
as the standard.
This blind approbation and self-serving admiration,
made death-dealing and concealing horrific
dismantling society for private gain
a most appropriate conduct.
Throughout three and half centuries
Liars, cheats, and thieves maintained

these behaviors without the measure of few pieces
of accountability crashing down upon their heads.
They cultivated their own system of skillful protection,
loosening the courts, bribing law enforcements,
launching marketing deception
that targeted specific individuals or groups.
Other key foundational elements of the grand society
fell under their twisted imagination.
Behold power and control,
the true enemy of the soul,
which estranged the U.S.
We are nothing more than a pest, a pet of the entitled
who truly manage the world for their self-serving,
land, silver, and gold.
They easily avoid caring and will choose
slight if any adherence to the face
and heart of justice, freedom, and equality.

REPULSIVE LIFESTYLE

Too much was what left them ravaged.
Cooked, sold on the hot spit.
The long -drawn stillness questioned
the arrival of the mockingbird's plight
whose flight cursed their misshapen love.
From the silver goblet the red wine flowed,
toast after toast like continuous boasting
glorying the former loves, their eyes desired.
The pages of history tired; they had become worn.
The recipe no longer worked
to define right from wrong.
The icy winter stood a wall in their way
with a strained voice loaded with abject dismay.
Prayer after prayer had much to say
but encountered solely a cancerous remorse.
This stage in life retreated dishonorably, shamefully.
A divorce hanging from a desiccated tree.
Four years labored in wrangling defiance.
The end, now bleached, turned milky-white
is an unpleasant sight.
Disarmed by the weighted down proof
found in their perplexed destructiveness.
The repulsive lifestyle they lived
in their "Garden of Earthly Delights".

HOG HEAVEN

Hate has come.
It is here burying itself
day and night
in the canyon of my bedeviled soul.
The gnawing scrapes and scrapes
pealing what there is of a fated twisting vision.
I feel the belly's bottom churn,
Its undersection adjourns, erupting, repeating
chunks of caustic content.
They traverse over lower lips.
I expel deep conflicted breathing
that chart a premeditated course of action.
Aggravated anger speaks
to me in varying degrees of rage.
Life is being questioned.
Life has become devalued
at the discretion of force simply beckoning.
Four letters escape and punctuate
the torment dwelling in the mind.
It is a sign that re-aligns the stars
by which I am deeded to follow.
The march to freedom
is the march to halt forever total rejection.
Better is death than a pig's life swirling in hog heaven.

MUTATION

87

Sad we are to have ceased really communicating.
Nothing was anymore.
Our time is spent sweeping dirt from the floor.
A butler or maid managing the house, its owners
speak hours to other strangers about.
Pride is the true disconnect
between that haves and have not.
There is a multi-spatial distance in the austere feelings
roaming the floor space of the official temple.
How did essential discourse
displace their world with sparce dramatic lack of use?
Touching became a fearful sickness,
a frightening disgust,
a galling liability which endorsed a surging rigidity.
The verbal tug of war in their residence
resounded off the walls.
The animals themselves barked and sought shelter
beneath tables and chairs,
sometimes fleeing up the stairs.
The qualms made use of spiritual psalms afterwards.
Adjustment switched to replacement,
A modification
before his reversal could remodel the addition
of her bleak distorted mutation.
What good is the heart's love
if it can't stand firmly
and obey what it most should trust?

ABOUT THE HOUSE

Our house was a near perfect place
until it came to be erased.
Soft songs within played to herald the crispy mornings
and late cool evenings as they sat
on the circular wooden porch,
a cup of herbal tea resting in their palms.
Man and woman accepted the hunger for more
and cheered all they had to spare.
Adoration in times of mutually shouldered compliments
were stored by the bushel.
The silver looking silo overflowed.
The game of fortune never tested
until age began resisting
and crowded the creaking house.
The wobbling outer frame indicated
the flag was being lowered.
Its vitality devoured.
Fire leaning through found everywhere
to shower its "dog day afternoon".
Red eyes searched but were scattered
like a sand pebble swatted in a vociferous hurricane
from which they made haste to escape.
The end attacked them,
eating the panels of their fine dwelling.
Its character fell apart.
No hunger remained on the sidewalk.

No red, blue, and white flowers stood as an invocation
to refinement's masterful trapping s or ode recalling
what and where they shared a "quantum of solace."
The venue superior for a dance to experience the day
unfortunately, had been abandoned
for the pursuit of crass delusions.
Their love song unplugged,
between them inherited a casual shrug
indicating a faulty, this or that.
Glazed over eyes also said, "so what"
as the hammer crashed their poor star-cross country- party.

SPIRITS

I lay in bed and feel myself crying.
I am a man of many scores
But where is she, my mother, the one soul
I truly adored.
She was well-being, my repose.
The safety, I need not implore.
In life change comes and returns again
until we reach our end.
Do we call it a friend at the last moment taken?
The truest of all things are the thoughts that remain.
The thoughts which fill, without complaint.
Yet she too left as time changed.
What was I to do?
Simply continue.
Though a vessel emptied of ballas,
strangling, dangling from the yardarm,
I resisted joining the ocean
that would welcome me
as it does all sea farers
committed to its merciful deep.
Temporary tears lingered.
They are the love I feel for you, mom,
Perhaps they follow me from your spirit above.
Are these spirit drops, another chance?
An apparition would suffice.
Later that night when sleep arrived,

she touched my arm.
Outside the window, the clouds formed her portrait.
Words of solace displayed themselves.
From her lips she said, "son I will always love you."
"cry if you must but stay true to love."
"It will lead you to me and I to you will follow
to set your heart free of its pain."
"Together we, together to be"
"God to us we trust,
though our bodies are far apart
our spirits, are never ajar."

DEVIL'S CHARM

The devil brought malady and agony
into the home of purity
He guided fools, interrupting their minds.
They were befuddled, bewildered by his disguise.
Taken for an adulterous ride.
Pride encountered hardly scoffed.
The glory of the country fell short of its foundation,
stricken from core values which were stolen.
Many, like in the annals before
were herded into pens to be slaughtered.
The ghouls are frightening whether in uniforms or suits.
They shoot; they kill at will.
Respect for life is forbidden.
The thrill that power brings
casts its own absolute thrill
like drunkenness exposing the inclination to boast
when blood streams along the sidewalk
as bodies flip-flop like fish hauled to the shore,
left there to choke and die.
The acolytes wanted desperately to believe
in their new God.
He who is the devil in disguise.
They preferred the seal of influence without culpability.
Blame or responsibility had shame attached
from the start of their hideous journey.
Deny, deny, project anger and disregard at someone

use insolence as a cover for gross impudence.
We need an island for those wishing
to divorce charity from themselves,
divorce mercy while sleeping with the Mongol hordes.
The republic lives in hell.
The devil has its residing taxpayers
under his insidious charm.
The callous minority raises no alarm.
Our mouths and stomach cannot afford to stay calm.
Scream or die (vote), we must,
in this river of scandalous disgrace.

FUTURE'S GIFT

Dad worked hard every day.
Mom gave a hundred and fifty percent.
Side by side they knew what was needed
to keep the family from falling through a terrible gap
that would snatch the very life from our chest.
We would perish instantly,
if they didn't wake each morning,
walk to work,
tighten their fists,
strengthen their backs,
bruise their knuckles,
not sit down on the ground.
They had to bring home a smile as well.
This would tell the fib,
shielding the requirement
for the trend to happen all over again
like spokes fortifying the contour of the wheel,
allowing its circular motion to succeed.
The two boys saw the daily effort
and grew to respect what it acquired,
food, electricity, water, and a bed to sleep on.
The ode that described
their start of day and close of night.
Their parents were two loving heroes.
Giants, Titans willing to go head on with brutes
named, the price of rice, vegetables, fish, and foul,

on Sunday, a treat to the beach.
Dad and Mom guaranteed we, the family could live
in today and have another chance at tomorrow.
They finally paid for giving us (boys) possibilities,
with their lives,
their deaths,
their hope,
their strength,
with their future, we, the sons, rented.

ABOUT THE AUTHOR OF VIRUS

Stephen James Pitters' spontaneity employs the conscious and the unconscious as he works his way through the past in varying degrees of reflection. His honest expressions and his unbridled emotions provide the reader with a sense of intimacy and invites them into his and the America's histories where interracial relationships salted often with violence, imprisonment, and even death. His poems have a specific nuance, yet they take calculated risks of exposing his innermost thoughts. He uses sentiment without being sentimental.

Pitters writes in the people's words without reliance on corporate and academic styles or formulaic conventions so pervasive in contemporary poetry. He uses the politics of emotions. How lovers plot to embrace or to escape their entanglements.

Stephen Pitters has sold hundreds of books of his collections from California to Washington.

Pitters holds master's degrees in clinical social work from Simmons School of Social Work, Boston Massachusetts (1972-74) and University of Pittsburgh School of Public Health. (1977-79)

He taught stress and anger management, couples communication, parenting, and marketing.

- He has a Teaching Certificate from Gonzaga University.
- His first book was *Bridges of Visions* (Gribble Press, 2009)
- The second one was *Walks Through the Mind* (Gribble Press, 2011)
- The third one *Currencies of Life and Enlisted Behaviors* (2013)

Pitters hosts The Spokane Open Poetry Program on KYRS Thin Air Community Radio since 2004. Stephen produced *Poetry Rising on the Northside* at Spokane libraries and has provided poetry, prose, and music events for senior centers in Spokane, Washington.

Six of his poems have been made into songs by California singer songwriter Traci De Leon. Musical compositions by Poise Kalin, and jazz musician Jermaine Carlton are composed for his poems. His works have also been made into visual art pieces by local artists, Megan Perkins, Tracy Poindexter-Canton and Kenyan batik artist Nicholas Sironka, Madison Throop, Art Jacobs, Halle Kuhar-Pitters, Sculptor James McLeod. A quilt and pottery piece were presented by Karen Owsley, Mimi Sproul, and Teresa Brynestad, respectively.

He performed poetry readings for local libraries in the area and at local high schools. He recently gave presentations for Black History Month at three different libraries using his own ancestry, which he traced directly back to 1807.

Conversations on Altered Roadways (2017) and *Prerecorded* (2018) are his latest manuscripts and are part of a five- part series vested in an age-related timeline theme.

The next contribution was *The Eye of the Spirit* (2019) followed by *Contesting* (2020). His works can be found on Amazon.com, Kindle and at local bookstores in Spokane.